For Alice, Kenny and Dale

Are you SURE you want to post that?

Smart Social Networking

Published by:
The Power of Laughter™
3439 NE Sandy Blvd. #104
Portland, OR 97232
www.thepoweroflaughter.com

ISBN: 978-0-9728783-1-9

Contributing Editors: Audrey Hand, Susan Cronewett

Cover Photography: Susan Cronewett

Copy Editors: Joey Volschenk, Cara Stein

Photography: Gail Hand

Manufactured in the United States of America
First Edition

Contents

Special Thanks To

Rich DiGirolamo for your brilliant mind, creativity love and prodding – you are the best fake husband a girl could never have.

Amy Lyndon for your sisterly friendship, encouragement and cheerleading expertise.

Christine Knight for your continued friendship and rescuing amazing dogs in *Murray & Archie*. I love you all so much.

Jennifer Powers, you are a guiding force to the light of universal happiness. No really I mean it! Rock on sis.

Valerie Carsey – your support, creative & critical mind is a true blessing. Go take over the world!

Judy and Ilan, thank you for finding my amazing dogs and your inspiration over the years.

Joshua Waldman, I adore you and appreciate all your support and guidance – go get a tattoo already!

Susan Cronewett, your graphic brilliance, culinary flair, love for animals and humor are truly inspirational.

Each college administrator that encouraged me to write this book – let's get this party to online peace started!

And lastly a very special thanks to Zippy and Zoe, my sweet, beautiful dogs. You brighten every moment of my life and remind me to spread laughter and kindness online. You've also taught me that on the internet, dogs' opinions matter too.

I hope *@pupinions* continues to have more followers than *@gailhand* on *Twitter* (rotten dogs).

Foreword

The media seems hell-bent on ruining my fun online. In just this last week, the following troubling headlines popped my social media bubble:

- *Teenage girl posts picture of cash on Facebook, family robbed within hours.*
- *Facebook, Google Less Trusted Than Your Grocery Store*
- *13 People Who Got Fired For Tweeting.*
- *Without Social Media, 18% Of Teens Would 'Stop Communicating'*
- *Fan Booted From Concert for Negative Tweet.*

With this kind of coverage, it's no wonder so many people are freaking out about what to do about *Facebook*, *Twitter* and *LinkedIn*. (And if they're not freaking out, they haven't been paying attention!)

Sure, the media thrives on fear, and many of these cases are outliers. But the stakes are still pretty high. Your career, your reputation, your friendships are all vulnerable. In many cases, it just takes one stupid post to ruin a college career, family relationship or career opportunity.

But through a little education, you'll be able to relax and use these networks for what they were intended for, to connect and interact authentically.

The first step in this process begins with a mindset shift.
You see, despite how easy it is to post, or fill out profiles, when you use social media, you are essentially a publisher.

Change your mind-set to that of a publisher. Think, **"My Facebook page is my publishing medium"**.

The problem for many people is that they don't have experience publishing or being publishers; and so how to 'do' social media right remains nebulous.

This book, Smart Social Networking, is a great entry-point for stepping into the mind of a publisher. It will show you how to think about your audience, decide on what to say and what not to say. There's even a chapter that will help your career.

So if you would like to avoid a social media disaster, take Gail's advice to heart.

Joshua Waldman, MBA, Author of Job Searching with Social Media for Dummies.
Portland OR
July 20th, 2012

Introduction

This book was written for the public persona in all of us. As Joshua pointed out in his **Foreword** - we are media. That said, I've created some simple tips to follow for you to become a Smart Social Networker online.

This will make it easy to keep your tweets, texts and posts out of tabloid headlines and keep your life and career - drama free and joyous.

We all like to have some fun online – but at what cost? These simple tips will teach each one of us to thoroughly think every keystroke through before clicking post or send.

In the liberal land of Social Networking, censorship is not something any of us want to practice or adhere to. I don't like it either –believe me – but sometimes it's better to be safe than sorry.

Adhere? Are you kidding? Yes, like glue – in fact how about the next time, before you go post something spontaneously, you glue your hands to the side of your keyboard or phone and read the following tips in this book.

In our application centered electronic society it is easy to just blip out some raw feelings with no thoughts about the long-standing ramifications. However, there are 4 generations on your campus and out in the work force where you someday hope to be employed or share your entrepreneurial brilliance. The people hiring you can be any age, sex or nationality, which leaves plenty of room for you to offend a future employer with random postings.

This is one more reason why you need to think before you post. Years from now, next month or even next week, you need to be prepared to defend your actions.

Just ask the student in NC who trashed his school online after finishing his finals. He caused a commotion and a huge debate ensued in his town. He barely got to graduate with his class.

What was he thinking? He wasn't, that is clear.

Impulsivity and spontaneity are great for last minute road trips. However, where it concerns Social Networking, your last minute thoughts may become the volatile words that remain ingrained on the **World Wide Web** forever.

Chapter One

Humor Rules Online

Ok, let's get to it:

Just like telling jokes, when you post comments you want to avoid any form of slander:

- Sexism
- Racism
- Gender Bias
- Mentally Challenged
- Religion
- Political Slander

Which of course leaves you with nothing to joke about, right? The highest form of humor is self-deprecation, so if you are going to make fun of someone and don't want to offend anyone – make fun of yourself!

Comedians such as: Jason Segal, Melissa McCarthy, Paul Rudd, Ellen and Seth Rogan have mastered this technique.
Comedians are experts at expressing their point of view during their sets.

Similar to the opportunity you have every time you post something online. Some have aversions to filters, which makes them righteous artists.

A good example of an artist with a strong POV[1] is Sarah Silverman. A few years ago Sarah offended a religious symbol aka Jesus. She got called to the carpet and had to explain her opinion.

---

1 Point of View

Be ready to explain your POV anytime you post something controversial. It may be years from now, but know that people will judge you. The more comfortable you are with explaining your actions, the less trouble you will have down the road.

When it's time to interview, date or change careers and your name is googled you might find yourself in the position of explaining your thoughts from years ago.

If you are an athlete and planning to take your sport on as your profession, you are most likely already familiar with the online paparazzi you have to deal with, especially on sites such as *Twitter* and *Facebook*.

If you are dating someone, they have the opportunity to embarrass you more publicly than someone whose profession doesn't place him/her in the 24/7 limelight. So choose wisely!

In my hometown of Portland, Oregon, the *Trailblazers* acquired a great young basketball star several years ago. He was very popular with the ladies.

During their courtship, Greg Oden decided to send a picture of his private parts to his new girlfriend via text message.

This 'sexting' move may have seemed innocent at the time. However when they broke up she sent a blast out on the internet and it went viral very fast.

Greg had to face the consequences; he appeared on both local Portland news and then National news and had to apologize to Oregon and the NBA for his actions.

He said he had no idea that this would have happened. All he did was send a **private** text message to his girlfriend.

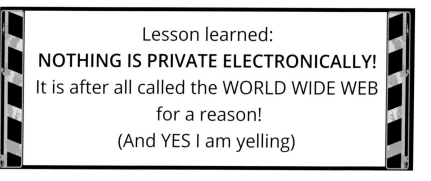

Lesson learned:
NOTHING IS PRIVATE ELECTRONICALLY!
It is after all called the WORLD WIDE WEB
for a reason!
(And YES I am yelling)

The Lone Banana

I'm no Hermione[2] when it comes to pictures that shouldn't go public, but this one was a doozie.

While in college, at the age of 21, Hilary took part in her weeknight music and beer party on campus. That specific evening it involved a banana-eating contest.

Being the fiercely competitive captain of the women's tennis team she wanted to win! Hilary glanced over at the Captain of the men's Basketball team and they nodded at each other knowingly. Game on!

They took their places on the stage and proceeded to make a scene. The crowd egged them on, until the point where he unzipped his pants and put the unpeeled banana through the zipper. Did I mention Hilary had been drinking?

The crowd went crazy. They won the contest – the result of their antics. Yes, Hilary peeled and ate the banana but not before she

---

2 Yes I am a Harry Potter fan – I own a wand!

saw a flash out of the corner of her eye. She popped up and saw a young guy with a camera and marched over to him. She told him that it was not okay with her to have him do anything with that picture. If it was a digital camera she could have forced him to delete the picture because it was her image.

The thought of suing him did not cross her mind, but it certainly does now! The young man was the editor of the college newspaper. He knew he had the opportunity to make fun of the jocks on campus with the photo. Despite her pleading with him not to publish it, he lied to Hilary, and told her he would bury the photo. He made it clear that she would not need to worry.

A week later on the front cover of the paper was a picture of her, on her knees. It didn't look good. She was horrified. For months after her life on campus became unpleasant; all the guys on campus were harassing her and the girls were embarrassed for her. It was a really difficult situation and she chose to 'solve' it by drinking more. Luckily Hilary had a good counselor on her college campus, who she credits to this day for saving her life and her sanity.

That was a campus of 8,000 people. What if it ended up on Facebook, Twitter or Instagram for 245 million people to share?

It was considered bullying then as it is now. Looking back on the event, Hilary told me she truly did not think that she would have survived the humiliation. She could easily have been another statistic of a young person embarrassed to the point of suicide like *Taylor Clementi*.

Her self-esteem was not that great in college around anything but the sports she excelled in.

I share this humiliating story with you because it was a low point in an important life that today could have easily been ended over a **PICTURE**. It took a lot of work for Hilary to get up and go on with her life.

Think about that the next time you want to post something you think is funny of a friend or acquaintance – it may affect them throughout their lives.

Is this action showing your true character?

Whether you answered yes or no continue to ask yourself these questions, if you have reasonably kind answers, by all means post away!

Can you ask yourself (from now on):

- *Who are you doing this for?*
- *Why are you really posting it?*
- *Are you trying to impress someone?*
- *Are you trying to send a message?*
- *Where will it go after going viral?*
- *Will it come back to haunt this person or you?*
- *Will you or the person in question ever regret the post?*

For the gamblers – go ahead take a chance.

Probability says it's not going to affect you for long if ever, just remember there is still the **possibility** that it might.

To be PC[3] or not PC, that is the question.

A few years ago I was on tour in the Midwest and a student came up to me after my program and wanted to use my microphone to share a new comedy piece he wrote for the students. I was done, so I handed him the microphone.

He had a character that slurred and either sounded drunk or mentally ill. I watched his peers cheer and egg him on. This continued for about 5 minutes when he handed the microphone back to me with a smile saying; *"I hope someone posts that on YouTube!"*

I was horrified. I have a brother who is mentally ill and found his comedy rather offensive. Yet the crowd loved him or did they really? I wonder how many of those students were laughing at him instead of with him.

It really didn't matter, I just felt as a humor professional I needed to let him know that at some point this comedy would offend someone and he needed to be prepared for it, especially online. I delivered the news; he thanked me and went on with his life. If he ends up with a sitcom, it probably won't last long. I don't think it is 'cool' to make fun of someone who isn't capable of defending him or herself.

If someone who is mentally challenged invites you to laugh **with them**, then it is safe and p.c. If not, save yourself the grief and be a politically correct poster; in the long run everyone will respect you more.

- *Defend your POV and you can get past a bad post online.*
- *Know it may take a while and it might not be very comfortable.*
- *You'll lose some friends and fans and gain others.*

_____
3 Politically Correct

> **Note:**
> You may also want to avoid talking
> about *Jeremiah Weed* & *Hairy Buffalo* online.
> People will understand they are
> not real people but rather substances.

Tweets that are NOT advised...

- *I'm thinking hairy buffalo for lunch.*
- *Swimming in the back of a truck with the football crew and hairy buffalo.*
- *Hairy buffalo during the day and a _____ (fill in your school's abbreviation) game tonight – stoked!*
- *The inventor of the hairy buffalo needs to be punched right now; my head hurts.*

This status update is also under 140 characters, so choose if you'd post this update:

I'm really drunk and I'm about to make a fool of myself by doing something illicit or illegal. Please take my photo – just kidding.

Personal Workbook 1

Write down the strangest *Tweet* you have seen lately?

```

```

Write down the most inappropriate *tweet* you've seen?

```

```

Was it written by someone you respected?

```

```

If yes, how do you feel about them now?

```

```

Chapter Two
Yes they are watching you!

Tip #1

There are the 5 questions I want you to consider the next time you post.

Put your hand up right in front of your face like this.

Hand's Up

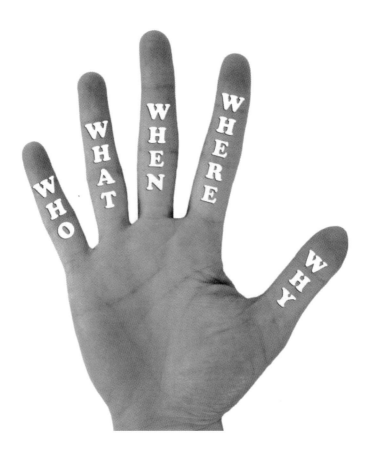

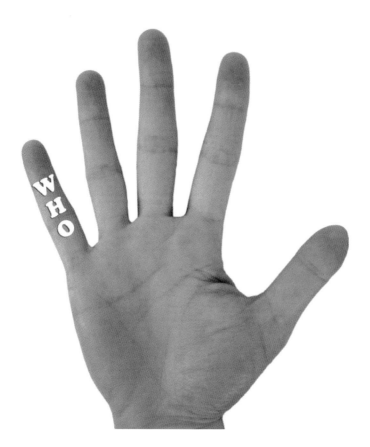

The 1st question:

Who is going to see this... have you asked yourself this question before you post?

a. Yes, I have asked the question.
b. No, it's not on my radar.
c. I don't care who sees what I post.
d. Why does this matter?

If you answered **(d)** you will be happy to know the teacher who was writing an email to a friend about not looking forward to another year at her school with the (insert superlative) students; needed to ask herself this before she posted.

So did the student who was a star football player *tweeting* negative chatter about his opponent. He felt he was immune to judgments.

They were wrong.

The teacher lost her job after being a well-respected and admired educator of 35 years.

The second was banned from the field for 6 games and he lost his team playoff rights.

It mattered!

Here is a 2nd question about WHOM:

What were you about to post the last time you really thought about WHO was going to see your post before you posted it?

a. Something nasty about someone I have or haven't dated.
b. A random thought about a campus issue or teacher.
c. A comment about a party.
d. A comment about a roommate.

Personal Workbook 2:

Do you think that you've ever hurt someone via a post?

○   Yes, for sure.

○   No, I am pretty kind to people.

○   Maybe, I have never really thought about it

What did you write?

[ ]

Have you ever apologized or made amends?

○   Yes

○   No

○   I am considering it now that I have been reminded.

Think of some other people you may have offended, online, over the past few years.   Is there anyone else you may want to apologize to?

[ ]

What did you write that could have been offensive or upsetting to that person or group?

Are you surprised at how many people you may have angered?

○ Yes
○ No

Look up 2 or more of your friend's pages on both *Twitter* and *Facebook*. Find a few comments that need to be deleted and list them here:

Friend's name:

Facebook:

Twitter:

Friend's name:

Facebook:

Twitter:

Additional Notes:

When you realize you've made a mistake, make amends immediately. It's easier to eat crow while it's still warm.
~Dan Heist

Chapter Three

Feel like sending a nasty text?
Go take a walk

Tip #2

Ask yourself...

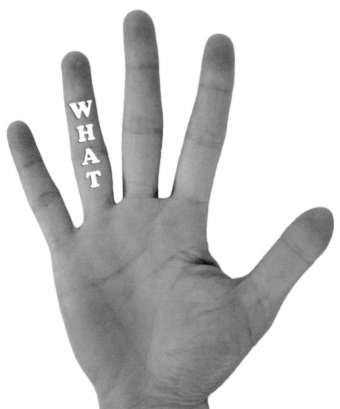

What is your motivation?

Presently, many of us would much rather send a text, an email or connect with someone online. Seriously, if you don't have unlimited texting, what good is the phone?

What about drunken texting? Also known as 'drexting'[1]. This was known as drunken dialing when your parents were younger.

_____

1 Yes I created this word, feel free to use it.

The difference?
Most of those calls were not recorded!

When you're feeling angry, jealous or vindictive it is **NOT** a good time to text or post your feelings online. Remember everything you write is being logged somewhere.

There is a simple software program that jealous lovers buy to decode text messages. The evidence can be used in divorce cases as well as in criminal investigations as we've all seen in CSI.

What was the last inappropriate text you sent or received?

Don't people need to know how I feel?
I'm just trying to express my emotions!
A very good point, however...

Locations to avoid angry postings:

1. The person's wall on *Facebook, Google+* etc. you may be angry at.
2. Your own wall
3. *Twitter*
4. A blog – your own or the school's.

> If you are not prepared to post it on a billboard
> for everyone to see - don't post it online.
> That is your litmus test and they are only
> your partial
> audience, as we both know!

**Have the courage to pick up the phone and talk to
someone about why you are upset.
Ask if you can meet them in person.**

Reading a facial expression online, via email or text is impossible. We all know you can't decipher emotion via emoticon.

At the very least have the courage to have a *Skype* conversation with person in question; it's the closest you'll get to meeting face to face.

Strong emotions are misinterpreted and leave little to the imagination when you involve social mediums such as; texting, email or 140 characters on *Twitter*.

Face to face can be challenging, so role-play with a friend for practice, it helps!

Go take a walk, chill and calmly deal with your object of anger. It's much easier than upsetting someone publicly and having to deal with other people's judgment of your emotions.

Remember whose watching your posts... Anyone and everyone can view your posts for years to come.

Being appropriate with your emotions can save you a lot of grief online and in the long run. Just ask the student in NC who started trashing his school online after finishing his finals and barely got to graduate with his class.

What was he thinking? He wasn't, that's clear.

Ratemyprofessor.com was designed for students to have an outlet to let their professors know how they are doing.

Did you ever really think it was anonymous?

It's not hard to trace a post if it proves to be defamatory to the professor. Think long and hard about your words before you voice your true thoughts. Is there a way in which you can be heard but not overly mean or nasty?

Personal workbook 3

Look at your last 3 posts on *Facebook, Twitter, Foursquare, Google+, Instagram* or wherever else you post.

Write each of them down and think about your motivation while you answer this; what were you trying to accomplish?

This is what I posted:

```

```

What was I trying to accomplish?

```

```

Do this 2 more times, and then review a few of your friend's posts. Try to guess what their motivations were.

This is what I posted:

```



```

What was I trying to accomplish?

```



```

This is what I posted:

```



```

What was I trying to accomplish?

```



```

Now move on to your friends, a coach or a teacher to see the difference in their social networking style.

This is what I posted:

What was I trying to accomplish?

This is what I posted:

What was I trying to accomplish?

**If you see anything defamatory remember
to be kind and point it out to your peers.
They may not thank you now,
but eventually they will.**

Chapter Four
Viral Schmiral – who cares?

Tip #3
Ask Yourself...

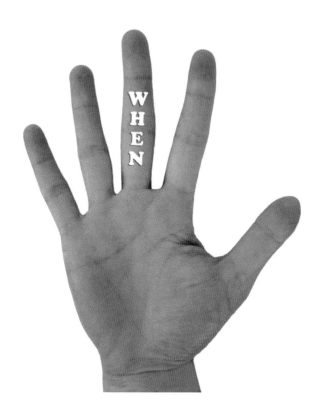

When could it come back to haunt you?

It's true, athletic teams and administration who grant scholarships to students evaluate your online profile and decide whether they can trust you with your freedom of speech (really).

In the past year in my travels I have spoken to over 1500 administrators across the country. Almost a dozen of those schools have revoked athletic scholarships over improper social network postings.

Is that unnecessary roughness?
If you have any doubts about whether your post will offend, don't post it.

Here are examples of when compromising photos can return to haunt you.

1. *Job interviews*

2. *Grad school interviews*

3. *Potential people you want to date, marry or have a relationship with.*

4. *Your significant other, parent, coach or boss doesn't need to know you went out when you said you were ill.*

5. *Underage drinking – whether you are doing it or simply attending the party, there are states where you can be held responsible.*

6. *If you are a teacher or coach. You are in a position where students look up to you. Avoid posting photos of yourself drinking. It really doesn't matter that you are 21. No one is telling you not to drink, just have the discretion to not post it online.*

7. *Until Marijuana is legalized, no bongs or joints or any other modern smoking device photos of yourself or friends online should be posted.*

Ask **Michael Phelps** for advice on this one.

Tip #4

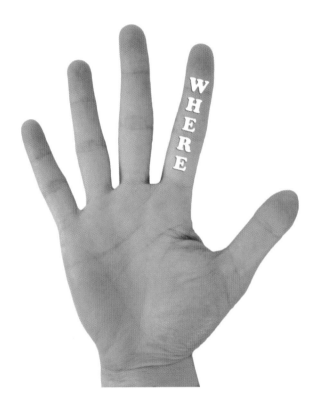

Ask Yourself... If this goes viral where will it go?

The answer is simple; everywhere and anywhere. You don't control social media. *Google's* algorithms get better every year; there is no hiding from the big G.

While growing up, anonymity and scruples were the words my parents used when they taught us about privacy. As old fashioned as it sounds, there is nothing wrong with passing the concept on to you – the next generation of great thinkers.

> **Bottom line one more time:**
> If you are not willing to stand up in the middle of your campus and announce what you are posting, chances are it doesn't need to be online. It would be better off kept within your close circle of friends.
> Do not post it. It's that simple.

It's a challenge to keep one's life private these days, but it is possible to refrain from social media for many people. Face to face conversations are one of the nicest ways to connect with other people.

There are 245 Billion *YouTube* and *Twitter* members as of summer 2012. This makes possibilities endless if the picture or post is juicy enough.

If you want to be smart about your future or current career stick to *LinkedIn*. It is a great way to develop your online reputation, work history and network with potential employers.

LinkedIn

In my opinion the best book currently available on the subject of social media is by the author who wrote my forward; Joshua Waldman.

Josh has some great tips about professionalism on *Linked In* and why it's so easy to network effectively. You have a head start while still in school and can easily connect with people sharing your future profession.

To create your *LinkedIn* profile:
a. A simple biography
b. Add your summer jobs, internships and volunteerism
c. State your career aspirations.

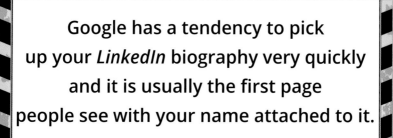

Google has a tendency to pick up your *LinkedIn* biography very quickly and it is usually the first page people see with your name attached to it.

So who are your bff's online anyway?

Some thoughts on managing your Custom Safety Settings and privacy on Facebook:

If you haven't changed your safety settings in the past year you are missing out on some good opportunities to limit your audience.

Most students I survey in an audience of 300 that I am speaking to, there are about 75% who have taken the time to lock down their customize safety settings on *Facebook*. For the rest of you, please think through whether your popularity ratings will suffer if you limit your audience online. Probably not.

If you are sharing settings are on Everyone:

This is the easiest way for Google to pull up your content in searches. Unless you are very clear about your goals, don't use this one unless you are already a rock star in college and want everyone to know everything you do and everything people say about you.

If you are sharing settings are on Friends and Networks:

This setting means companies and friends of friends will see all of your content, still not very safe if you want to get racy online with a few comments and photos.

If you are sharing settings are on Friend of Friends:

It is exactly what is says, but how well do you know all of your friends, friends? Do you like them, trust them?

If you are sharing settings are Friends only:

Simply put, the best decision today, unless you are a company promoting your business, band, comedian, etc.

Note: These days many college athletes obtain large fan bases during their college careers. With both *Twitter* and *Facebook*, it's important to think about your words and safety settings. Remember that your information can go viral faster than the average college student. Your *Heisman* or *Olympic* team awaits you.

Don't give the media something negative to work with. Keep them focused on your athletic achievements. This is one of the reasons you got that scholarship, right?

My advice is to lock down your settings in *Facebook*, if you haven't already, you won't be sorry.

PS - Don't forget to check your Wall Posting security – you have a chance to regulate your viewership on a regular basis there as well.

Athletes, focus on practice, getting good grades, volunteering in your community with your team and your sport.
This will keep your reputation solid!
Many of you will be leaders in your field, and this focus will pay off!

Tip # 5

Ask Yourself

What are you trying to accomplish?

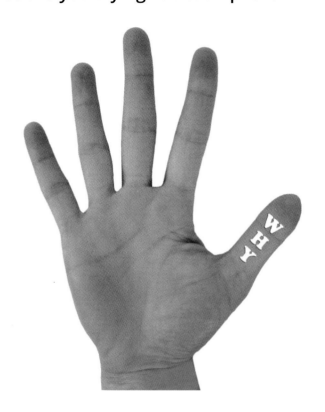

Is it for a good reason?

Asking yourself for a second time (from a different perspective) what your motivation is; can be a foolproof way of making sure that you understand what consequences your actions may bring.

- Are you trying to be unique?
- Do you want to share compelling information?

You can also apply the **WHY** are you posting this question to sharing your personal information on the web.

Just like they told you in your college Orientation – avoid posting the following:

- Cell Phone number
- Address
- Full Birthdate
- School Name
- Invitations to underage drinking parties.

It had to be said. The last one is just an invitation to add an incident to your school record. It won't benefit you or your future at all.

There are too many cyber criminals and stalkers you want to avoid handing too much information. Once it's out there it is logged somewhere. Just do your best to clean your profile up now, today.

AWESOME EMAIL ADDRESSES:

Are you using any of the following email addresses (or something similar) for your email address?

sexycoed@hotmail.com
beerbongchamp@gmail.com
nakedstud@gmail.com
drunknkitty@hotmail.com

I could list 1,000s of these hysterical names. They may make you laugh, but they are not funny when they come up in a Google search associated with your name.

When it comes to employers digging up information about your online life, this might be enough of a reason to reject you!

Since you haven't worked for these companies and have a limited work history, they look for information about your character online.

You will be defined as a **character** that is guaranteed. But you probably won't get an immediate call or interview for a job or grad school invitation.

Changes I need to make after reading this chapter:

Chapter Five
Why be kind online?

I've got your back Chippy, do you have mine?

- Would your friends or colleagues tell you if they saw something offensive about you online?

- Would they voice their opinions if you crossed the line (verbally) online or in an email that you shared with them?

If you answered **NO** to these questions, it's time to do something about this right away.

Like bad news and sometimes good news – messages, texts, emails, posts, *tweets*, pictures, videos etc. spread extremely fast. It is beyond our control to anticipate what will upset someone.

Having a buddy who has your back can keep you from falling prey to the 'open-mouth-insert-foot-syndrome'. It might even salvage your chance to engage in business with someone.

Personal workbook 3

Who has your back online?

It's good to have a backup, so list two here:

Friend's name

Friend's name

Again, we all have our own opinions and we can share them. However, we need to remember that at some point (in our online postings); we are going to upset someone.
It is almost humanly impossible not to.

I've been told that while
***Twitter* teaches you to fall in love with people you've never met—**
***Facebook* encourages you to admire and hate people you already know.**
—Anonymous

For instance; you told someone you were not going out of town and then you post a picture of yourself having a blast away from home. They see the picture and derive that you don't like their company (even if it was unintentional), you may have upset that person.

What about relationships?

Is it important to share your relationship status online?

If both people agree to share the status, then go for it! If you choose not to ask - you run the risk of upsetting the person you care about. If you aren't on the same page you risk losing all the momentum you've made thus far.

On the other hand there are occasions when people may post a status about their relationship because they don't want to talk about it. This applies to a positive or negative status.

Tip #6

Leadership

Time to get creative with the fingers

Focus on leadership qualities when you're posting.

Communicating with the world at the press of a button is a responsibility many of us didn't grow up with. The moment you opened your first laptop, touched your first keyboard or had your first phone in your hand you began your online life.

	1	2	3	4	5
Integrity	○	○	○	○	○
Clear Goals	○	○	○	○	○
Motivation	○	○	○	○	○
Respect	○	○	○	○	○
Kindness	○	○	○	○	○

How have you done so far?

On a scale of **1 to 5**, with 5 the being the highest level, how would you rate yourself on these human leadership qualities describing your online life with posting, texting and emailing? Don't forget *YouTube!*

 If you scored less than 16 you have some work to do.

Social Networking is not called Slander Networking for a reason. It's supposed to be about people connecting instead of disconnecting by posting nasty or antagonistic comments or photos. If you want to be a part of creating world peace, work on theses 5 qualities (see previous page).

Bonus: Compliment someone the next time you have an opportunity online. It's a nice thing to do in person or online. You get kudos from the universe; make yourself and the other person smile. It's free!

Did you know that in 2011 89% of employers started using social networks for recruiting!

This is another reason to prove to your future employer that they are hiring someone who has morals. Your online presence represents your character whether you like it or not.

I have many photos at home from college. Those pictures will never make it online, if they did I guarantee you that my career would not have taken off so fast.

If you are someone who loves the college experience and wants to try everything – there is **NO** reason to make it public knowledge.

Let's be really clear here:

It doesn't matter whether you are drinking out of a red, blue, purple or camouflage cup – people will assume that you are drinking! (yes, even without the ping pong balls).

If you post a photo from an event online, you will never be able to get it offline. It will be there to haunt you for years to come.

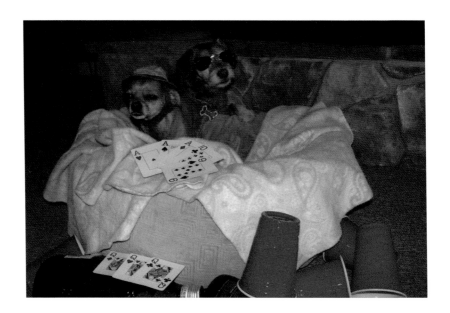

With photo recognition software, keeping your life private is going to get harder. I know some celebrities that like to lead more private lives. They have a 'check your phone in at the door policy', this avoids many misrepresentations.

There is nothing wrong with this rule and with photo recognition software I bet we'll see more and more opportunities to snap or be snapped in a scandalous picture, maybe even on campus!

Make sure you ask yourself the 5 questions:

Who, What, When, Where, Why

- If you can't come up with solid answers that make sense, remove the photos immediately. Save yourself the hassle.

- Do the same with your friends, if you see a photo online that can cause trouble – tell them!

- Be kind, it costs nothing and it's a great human leadership quality we can all strive for!

Life is about trying new things and having experiences. Remember that if you share those experiences privately not publicly, they will still be great experiences.

Not everyone needs to know your business. You too have paparazzi and as we know the paparazzi, they are not always kind and don't have our best interest at heart.

More often than not, they just want an interesting photo!

Thinking about your future career! How important is your job to you?

Chapter Six
Your future career awaits you

It may be time you take a second look at your online profile and **ALL** the content. In a recent study by Career Enlightenment these statistics were compiled:

- 1 of 3 employers rejected someone, based on something they found about them online.

- Over 2,000 people on *LinkedIn* have the same name as the top 10 people on the *FBI's* most wanted list.

- In 2011, 14.4 Million people used Social Networks to find their last job.

- 24% of Managers found 'fit and personality' from an online profile.

- 6 to 1 – The ratio of unemployed people to every job opening in America.

- 86% of employers say candidates should make their online profiles more employer friendly.

- 70% of job recruiters and hiring managers review an applicant's online information.

- 65% of companies have successfully hired employees using social media.

- 56% of HR professionals use networking websites to source potential candidates.

- 55% of companies plan on investing more in social recruiting this year.

- 50% of hiring companies plan to invest more in social recruiting.

Cleaning up your online profile:

1. Make sure you have a professional picture. It needs to be shoulder up, one you would send your Grandparents so they can show all their friends their collegiate grandchild they are so proud of they could *kvell.*

2. Go through your old *Facebook, Twitter, Foursquare and Google+* posts along with any *Instagram* pictures. Take down any posts that you believe may fit the 'inappropriate' category and delete them. Think; Grad School, Job, Political Office and your future kids will all be looking at these words. Even though these words may have represented your thoughts at the moment, ask yourself if they represent your public persona now. Does the content make sense for open distribution when you are ready to get an internship and job?

3. For fun go through one of your friend's posts and point a few out to them that they too could change or remove. We all have them once we change our perspective.

4. Update all your volunteer experience; it looks great on your résumé.

5. *Google* your name and see what photos or comments appear. Check the *Google* images search on more than one

browser. If you don't have anything negative appear in the first three pages, you are on the right track. However, if you don't like what you see in those first three pages you need to find the source and get that person to delete the images. That someone could be you!

6. Consult a student affairs administrator in your school if another student posted something that you don't like and refuses to take it down. Have them help you take legal action if you need to.

7. Beef up your *LinkedIn* profile. It is currently one of the best places to network.

8. If you do have something online and you have no idea how to remove it, try these tactics:
   Start blogging and it will get buried fast.
   Build an online profile for yourself on 25+ websites.

Thinking about your future career!
How important is your job to you?

Of all the companies surveyed[1]:
- 45% use *Twitter* to find talent
- 80% use *LinkedIn* to find talent
- 50% use *Facebook* to find talent

---

[1] Stats courtesy of the book Job Search with Social Media for Dummies by Joshua Waldman

Here are 20 to choose from to get you started.

Note: some may be gone by the time you read this... I did not list the 5 obvious sites; LinkedIn, Facebook, YouTube, Twitter and Google+

1. *Reddit*
2. *Simpy*
3. *Digg*
4. *Stumbleupon*
5. *Technorati*
6. *Magnolia*
7. *Zimbio*
8. *Jaiku*
9. *BlogCatalog*
10. *BlogMad*
11. *MyBlogLog*
12. *Hugg.com*
13. *LiveJournal*
14. *BlogSpot*
15. *ZippyVideos*
16. *Quizilla.com*
17. *Photobucket*
18. *Flickr*
19. *RememberTheMilk*
20. *WordPress*

Conclusion
THINK BEFORE YOU POST!!

More Ideas for cleaning up your online profiles from *CollegeMonster.com* **and** *About.com:*

During my College Leadership Conferences and programs many students ask me for the quickest way to delete negative

URL Code for you non-QR code techies: *http://college.monster.com/news/ articles/2144-take-control-of-your- online-image-how-to-wipe-it-clean*

information on the Internet.

This website, Monster College will teach you how to:
- How to Delete Friends on *MySpace*
- How to Delete your Usage History Tracks in Windows
  How to Recover Deleted Files from Your Computer
- How to Access Recently Deleted *YouTube* Videos
- How to Permanently Delete accounts such as, *Facebook*
- How to Restore Permanently Deleted Files from *Hotmail*

If you are already in college, the reality is that your exposure to social networking sites has increased exponentially. Whether nobly volunteering with your friends or team in your community, attending or hosting wild themed parties or random social activities your audiences will likely include:

- Admissions Staff
- Your new roommates
- Your personal stalkers
- Your professors
- Potential employers, both on and off campus
- Your RA (Residential Advisor)
- The campus judicial board (should you get in trouble)
- Campus and local police (should you get in trouble)

Here is another great source for deleting inappropriate *Facebook* photos:

URL Code for you non-QR code techies:
http://collegeapps.about.com/od/ theartofgettingaccepted/ss/bad-facebook-photos_11.htm

In my work with Student Life and Affairs in colleges they tell me the hardest part of their job is receiving that late night call they get to go to the local emergency room for a student who has alcohol poisoning from binge drinking.

From a college's perspective, there's nothing funny about it. Your friends may get a chuckle out of that picture of you hugging the porcelain throne, but a college official is going to think about the students who have died from alcohol poisoning, been raped while passed out, or choked to death on their own vomit.
Your application could easily end up on the rejection pile if a college admissions officer comes across such a photo.

Want to clean up your online image?

Check out *About.com's* 15 examples of *Facebook* photos that make you look good. I'll be creating some new examples soon which will be included in my next edition of this book, but you'll get the gist here.

http://collegeapps.about.com/od/theartofgettingaccepted/ss/good-facebook-photos.htm

Until then, think before you post and have fun online it's a great medium for communication and uniting the world when used with common sense and creativity.
PS - We all need to laugh more imho.

What action steps do you need to take to adjust your:

1. Safety Settings
2. Customized Settings on *Facebook*
3. Google photo's or posts that come up in the first three pages that are derogatory

Put your hand up and ask yourself the five questions. Do this every time regardless of the electronic device that you are using! Impulsivity online can ruin a reputation. And it could be your reputation first.

The Internet doesn't give you any do-overs.
Life isn't a dress rehearsal.
This is your life, your reputation, your well-being, your safety, your career and your love life.

- **What do you want it to look like in digital form?**
- **You deserve to have a great online reputation.**

Take the time to think before you post you'll be glad that you did!

Let us hear from you:

Send Gail an email about something you would like her to include in the next edition to **gail@gailhand.com** - We'll send you a cool sticker as a thank you.

Send us a message on *Facebook*: www.facebook.com/AreYouSureYouWantToPostThat

Follow Gail on *Twitter* **@gailhand** and let us know something you liked about the book.

If you don't have anything nice to say, I am sure you will send us a private email

And last but not least:

If you want to follow Zippy and Zoe, they are the true stars here, we both know it, **@pupinions** or on *Facebook*: *Zippyzoe.hand*

or

Catch them on their latest adventures online as pet consumer advocates on their *Rover Reporters* channel on *PetIndustryTV.com*